I0087552

Golden Star Publications

All Rights Reserved

Text Copyright 2019 by Virginia Ghoniem

ISBN Number: 978-0-692-11917-4

Publisher Number for Title Management is: 1891099

Dedicated to my father,
Roland G. Schink

Daddy, you will always be Daddy to me. You were home with us every day. The advantage of farm life is that dads and kids spend a lot of time together.

As a toddler, I spent hours watching you work, and then as I grew older, I spent even more time working next to you.

At the time I did not appreciate it as much as I should—particularly when we were milking cows or baling hay. But now I realize that the time we spent together was very special. Best of all, our house was filled with love and laughter, and, I will admit, a bit of complaining about doing the chores.

Why This Manual?

I've written this booked based on what I have witnessed through the years. My insight comes from personal experience as both a mother and a grandmother. But most importantly, it is based on what I observed for 15 years as a principal of large Los Angeles elementary schools.

Most parents, parent how they were parented.

In many situations it is the right way, in others, it may not have been the ideal way. This is not because a parent isn't wonderful, it is because they were parented in this fashion and do not know how to do it differently.

Many fathers were told they needed to be bread winners and believed that had to be their only focus. Taking care and spending time with the child was the work of the mother.

Times have changed and YOU need to break the cycle.

Knowledgeable fathers, like yourself, will be the ones who will make a tremendous difference for their children and for future generations.

It may seem hard to believe, but your actions will be mimicked and passed on for many generations. What you do with this child and your future babies will affect the future of the world.

Too many men do not view parenting as significant as their "real" job. But if you raise this child with the belief that this child has the same priority as your work, you will be shaping a bright future!

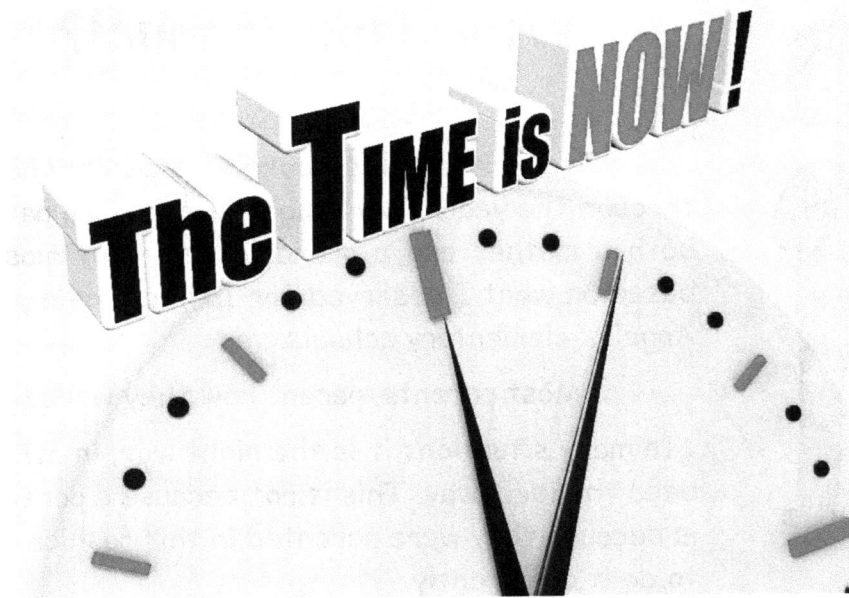
The Time is NOW!

Daddy-Time Tools

IT'S ONLY A MATTER OF TIME

SO

HAVE THE TIME OF YOUR LIFE!

Dads want to be a part of their children's lives, but many don't know what to do with children. Don't be surprised if mom feels the same. This little manual will give you a few ideas of what you can do to make the moments you spend with your child memorable for both of you. I know men like to believe that they know how to assemble everything without opening the instruction manual, but I am asking you to read this instruction manual for you and your baby.

It is also a good idea to re-read it occasionally. However, you won't be able to put this away for very long. Your child will grow and advance to the next level much faster than you expect, so be ready.

What do your children want most of all?

TIME!!!

How Do I Do This?

Men have many concerns when they are about to bring a child into the world. Traditionally, men worry that they will not have the means to take care of their new child. I will not belittle the fact that children are a huge fiscal responsibility, but to make a difference in your child's life, your greater responsibility is to help nurture your child into becoming a strong, functioning member of society.

The big question is, how do I accomplish this?

The answer: <u>Create</u> **time** to be with your child. Do not expect the time to magically appear. **<u>You have to make it happen.</u>**

If you have a super-busy schedule, which most people do now-a-days, you must actually calendar the time and make those appointments with your child as iron-clad and as unbreakable as the appointments you make with your colleagues at work.

The amount of time you spend with your child during the first four or five years of his/her life are essential to creating a happy, functioning child. The remaining 18 years that you will be spending with him/her is to <u>maintain</u> that successful and prosperous child. (Yes, you will be helping into his/her 20's!)

I don't mean that time with your child is difficult, it is NOT. You will love your child and love being with your child from the moment she/he is born. Each moment you spend will be unbelievably satisfying and rewarding, even when she/he keeps you awake all night.

The Informed Dad

Don't worry, children have survived un-enlightened fathers since the beginning of time. However, by reading this, you, who is a competent man, will be enlightened. A child is another extraordinary undertaking and a spectacular adventure.

The baby years will go by quickly. Soon, you will find your child entering elementary school. It may seem as if elementary school, middle school and high school are so far into the future that you cannot imagine them. But these are the years that "clock-in" before you know it.

Unfortunately, the elementary and teenage years is the time that people assume they do not need to prepare for. Therefore, fathers and mothers usually don't go looking for books to help them with these years. But you will soon learn that you do need to prepare for them. Many people, even women are afraid to ask for help because they believe parenting should be innate. It is not!

Before the child is born, parents look for books on what to do with the **baby**. People will give you ideas and advice for the baby—a newborn, —but the newborn stage lasts only a few months. It is a real challenge, especially if the child is your first. But the **time** you spend with your toddler, your child, **and your teenager** is as crucial, or more to your child's growth and success.

Yes, I will say it again and again.

The most important activity that you can do with your baby, your toddler, your child, and your teenager is to spend **TIME** with her/him.

Daddy Time
Tools

Infant
Time

Baby Banana Berry

The nine months that you are waiting for your little one to arrive seems endless. There is so much excitement and anticipation for everyone. And on top of that, future grandparents and friends are waiting for you to come up with a name for your little one.

You will find that the name you pick will truly embody your child's personality. Enjoy the process of picking a name. You may not want to share the actual name that you are thinking of until the "reveal" of the baby. This also gives you a chance to change your mind and puts a lot less pressure on the parents.

But you really must give your child a name while it is the womb. If you call it "baby" or "it" you are not making a real connection to the child. Give him or her a silly or whimsical name that makes you smile when you say it. You may want to call your unborn child: Junior, Homer, Pickles or perhaps Banana Berry.

For this instruction manual, I will name your child either Anthony or Cleopatra after the great ancient rulers. I am not trying to put pressure on your child to be a great ruler, but your high expectations for your children will help them set their goals high.

Infants

Yes, just as cuckoo clocks wake you up in the middle of the night, Cleopatra's seemingly constant crying will sound at all hours. Often you will find that her crying will chime on the hour, the half hour and sometimes on the quarter hour.

Your little one WILL grow out of this stage! Remember when you thought the pregnancy would never end? This is the same. You may think time is standing still and you will forever be in this sleepless stage but let me assure you—it gets better.

The Tool Box

You will not need to pull much out of your tool box when your child is an infant. You will need to use your hands, heart and head, (meaning common sense) for most of the time that your child is an infant.

There are very few THINGS that you will need. Books and CDs are the only tools you need, and I can guarantee there is someone in the family who will supply a constant stream of books. If for some reason, there is not a book giver, remember that Goodwill or the Salvation Army will have these books.

Cleopatra may not look at the book, or even seem interested. She most likely will grab at it or chew on it. However, your voice will soothe her, and you will be providing her a wealth of vocabulary words. We are still learning about the infant brain, so it is quite probable that she is absorbing much more than we think.

SUPER-DAD

The next component is not found in a toolbox.
It is in you!

Dad, you are superman to your child. But to be the super-hero your child needs, requires much more than physical strength. To be a super-dad requires stamina, inner strength, the ability to stay awake for long hours, and to be TRULY WILLING to help Mom get some rest.

Remember, she probably didn't sleep well the last couple months of her pregnancy. You try sleeping with a basketball in your belly and see how well you sleep.

How can you be the superhero she needs?

First, you must realize that Mom is taking care of Anthony all day long, nursing him, and changing him and holding and rocking and holding and rocking. Since she is so tired, it takes longer for her body to recover from the delivery. So...

Be a Superhero and heat up the milk in a bottle and let Mom sleep through the night at least twice a week. (Remember, if you are getting up twice, she is getting up five times, or more.)

How is this accomplished? Kiss Mom and IMMEDIATELY jump out of bed and ACT like this is something you _really want to do_. <u>Do not make her feel that you are doing her a great favor—remember, this is your baby, too.</u>

You may have to change the diaper. If you are not sure how to do this, please read the page in the manual on changing diapers. Then, **take the baby into the kitchen with you** to heat up the bottle.

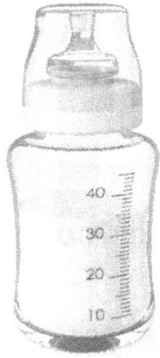

Preparation

If it is the weekend, and you are PLANNING on letting Mom sleep, she will gladly pump a bottle for two good night's sleep. If she has a few bottles prepared that are frozen, put one in the refrigerator to thaw before you go to bed.

Fill a four-cup measure about half full of water and place it into the microwave for about 1.5 to 2 minutes. Carefully take the cup out of the microwave (you don't want to burn Cleopatra) and place the bottle into the glass cup.

NEVER put a bottle with a nipple into the microwave. The nipple will be too hot and besides, heat and plastic do not mix well.

Keep a constant watch on the bottle because you never want it to get too warm. Check the temperature—**ALWAYS check the temperature**— by shaking a few drops of milk onto your inner wrist. The milk should **not** feel cold **or** warm and **never hot** on your wrist. It should be **room temperature**.

Get Comfortable!

Throw a burp bib or towel over your left shoulder, if you are right handed. This is essential. Then, sit in a comfortable chair, lay Cleopatra onto your left arm with her head resting in the crook of your arm. Gently touch her cheek on the side you wish her to turn, either with your finger or with the nipple.

Then, start by gently rubbing the nipple of the bottle on the baby's lower lip. Cleopatra will open her mouth and then hungrily take the nipple into her mouth. Hold the bottle so the milk always fills the nipple. If air gets into the nipple, then Cleopatra will get air into her tummy and then, believe me, the both of you will suffer. Cleopatra will get gassy and colicky and you will not get any sleep. The good news is that many of the newer baby bottles are made to prevent bubbles, but never totally rely on them.

Remember to stop half way through the bottle and burp her. Carefully, place her onto your chest with her head at your shoulder. Gently pat her back until you hear her burp. (She may not sound very lady-like at this point.) Also, sometimes babies spit up a little when they burp, don't worry, it is normal. This is why you keep the burp bib on your shoulder. Another way to burp her is to lay her across your lap, face down and gently pat her back. Once she burps, finish giving her the bottle and then burp her again. If Cleopatra is awake, make sure you make eye contact with her. If her eyes are closed, sit peacefully and enjoy the miracle in your hands.

Time for Mom

Mom is physically exhausted from childbirth and mentally exhausted from learning to be a mom and trying to be perfect at a job she is never done before. The most frustrating part is that John Q Public believes perfect mothering is innate and is a part of her DNA. It is not!!!

Let her know that you know how hard it is for her and you do not expect her to be perfect. But, believe me, that will not stop her from seeking perfection, because the **desire** to be perfect **is in her genes**.

Expect her to cry and/or be cranky because she feels inadequate, exhausted and frustrated that everything is not going as perfectly as she imagined.

BE PATIENT!

If you are not patient, Mom will be more stressed, the baby will feel her stress and your stress and....it all goes downhill from there. You don't want that to happen so smile and massage on!

Foot massage or back massage for mom.

If you need directions for a foot massage or a back massage, just ask Cleopatra's mother.

Back to Daddy—Time Tools for the Baby

Toe tickling, hand-holding and a baby massage.

You will be amazed when you watch Cleopatra's tiny feet curl in response to your gentle touch as you run your finger up the middle of her foot. Cleopatra loves to hear your soft voice while you are tickling her feet.

One **game** you can play is **"This Little Piggy"** as you wiggle her five toes with each stanza of the rhyme. You begin with her big toe which is tiny. "This little piggy went to the market, This little piggy stayed home, This little piggy had roast beef, This little piggy had none, And this little piggy went wee, wee, wee, all the way home." After you wiggle the last toe, run your fingers up her leg pretending that you are running home.

Hand holding--even though you never thought your fingers were particularly large, when you see that miniature hand with those tiny fingers wrapped around one finger, you will feel your power and a sense of awe over this little miracle. Suddenly, you realize this is your purpose in life, and that you are truly needed.

Baby massages. Take a **small** amount of coconut oil or Burt's Bees Baby oil, and gently massage your baby's back, legs and arms. Remember babies are NOT looking for a deep tissue massage. Make sure you use the baby oil, so you do not create too much friction when you are running your fingers over their muscles.

Changing Diapers

Everyday tasks help us get closer to the people we care about the most. And changing a diaper is an everyday task times 10! The good news is that a newborn diaper does not give off a foul odor. The bad news is that once your little one begins to take in food other than mom's milk, the waste product has quite a stench. But, remember, you are the "man" of the house! Your wife and child believe that you are so strong that you can fight dragons for them, so changing a smelly diaper is mere child's play for you.

The directions are quite simple. Lay Anthony on a flat surface, and on a spot on which he cannot fall off. For Anthony, you need to have a towel ready to place over his penis, so you are not given a surprise squirt in the face. Open the diaper he is wearing by pulling the tape tabs away from the front of the diaper. Place the towel over his penis. If Anthony is only wet, then gently wipe the baby's complete diaper area with a baby wipe or an already prepared wet washcloth.

If the diaper is heavily soiled, very gently use a clean portion of the used diaper to wipe away as much of the mess as you can. Then, you will need to use several baby wipes or a washcloth to clean Anthony's bottom, and entire diaper area. A baby has a lot of folds at the top of his legs and it is very important to get him clean everywhere. (There may be times when you will need to take Anthony to the sink and wash his bottom with warm (not hot) water and a gentle baby soap. Make sure you wipe the area completely dry. **You are not done—read on.**

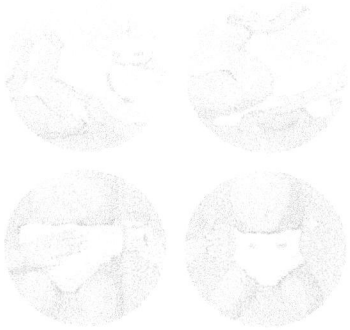

Diapers Galore

Diapers Some More

Have diapers readily available. You don't want to go looking for diapers at this pivotal moment. Pull the diaper out of the bag, box or wherever you have it stored, and open it a little so it will be easier to put on. Remember, keep the towel over his penis. Now, very carefully and gently, hold Anthony by the feet (his head should NEVER LEAVE the surface you put him on) and then slip the new diaper under his bottom with the tape tabs at the back.

You are almost there. Stay with us! Sometimes, if the diaper area is particularly red, you will need to rub some zinc oxide, more commonly known as paste for their butt, over the diaper area.

Finally, pull the front of the diaper up and gently place it between his legs. Open the tapes from the tab and then secure the tabs to the front of the diaper. Pay careful attention so you will not make the diaper too tight or too loose.

Sing a lullaby

Sing lullabies at night, early in the morning or late in the afternoon. A song will soothe both you and your little one. (It doesn't matter if you think you can't carry a tune, Cleopatra will think your voice is wonderful because you are her dad.)

Memorize a few of the lullabies on the following pages. Don't worry that you are not sure of the tune, Cleopatra will never know if many of your songs have the same tune. Cleopatra just needs your time and the sound of your voice to feel comforted.

You can find these lullabies on YouTube and sing along. Don't just play the YouTube video, Cleopatra needs to hear your voice—not just mom's voice, yours too.

Don't be a perfectionist with the tune, just sing!

Sing a Lullaby

Hush Little Baby

Hush, little baby, don't say a word.
Papa's gonna buy you a mockingbird

And if that mockingbird won't sing,
Papa's gonna buy you a diamond ring

And if that diamond ring turns brass,
Papa's gonna buy you a looking glass

And if that looking glass gets broke ,

Papa's gonna buy you a billy goat

And if that billy goat won't pull,
Papa's gonna buy you a cart and bull

And if that cart and bull turn over,
Papa's gonna buy you a dog named Rover

And if that dog named Rover won't bark
Papa's gonna buy you a horse and cart

And if that horse and cart fall down,
You'll still be the sweetest little baby in town

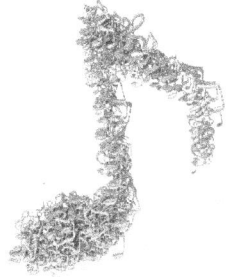

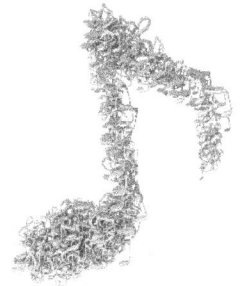

Day is Done

(Sung to the tune of taps)

Day is done,

Gone the sun,

From the lake, from the hills, from the sky,

All is well, safely rest,

God is nigh.

Rock a Bye Baby

Rock a bye baby, in the tree top

When the wind blows, the cradle will rock.

When the bough breaks, the cradle will fall,

And down will come baby, cradle and all.

Golden Slumbers

Golden slumbers kiss your eyes,

Smiles await you when you rise,

Sleep, pretty baby

Do not cry,

And I will sing you a lullaby.

Cares you know not,

Therefore sleep,

While over you a watch,

I'll keep.

Sleep, pretty darling,

Do not cry.

And I will sing you a lullaby.

Brahm's Lullaby

Lullaby and good night, with roses bedight

With lilies o'er spread is baby's wee bed,

Lay thee down now and rest,

May thy slumber be blessed.

Lay thee down now and rest,

May thy slumber be blessed.

Lullaby and goodnight, thy mother's delight

Bright angels beside my darling abide

They will guard thee at rest,

Thou shalt wake on my breast

They will guard thee at rest,

Thou shalt wake on my breast.

Sleep, Baby, Sleep

Sleep, baby, sleep

Your father tends the sheep

Your mother shakes the dreamland tree

And from it fall sweet dreams for thee

Sleep, baby, sleep

Sleep, baby, sleep

Sleep, baby, sleep

Our cottage vale is deep

The little lamb is on the green,

With snowy fleece so soft and clean

Sleep, baby, sleep,

Sleep, baby, sleep

Sleep, baby, sleep

All the Pretty Horses

Hush-a-bye, don't you cry, go to sleep-y little baby

When you awake you shall have all the pretty little horses.

Blacks and bays, dapple grays, coach and six white horses.

Hush-a-bye, don't you cry, go to sleep-y little baby.

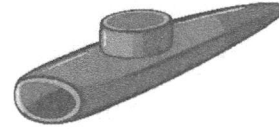

Play a guitar while singing

Take time during the next couple of months while you are waiting for Anthony to grow, to practice the lullabies. I am quite sure you have not played these before, but once you know the tunes, you will be able to use them for the next 10 years or more. Singing to your children makes a great bed time ritual. When you make this a habit your children will automatically relax and calm down when you begin to play. It also will relax you when your nerves are a little frazzled. Oh, and don't forget to play for mom. Mom can play the kazoo to accompany you or when Anthony gets older, he can play the kazoo with you.

Cuddle at every opportunity.

Holding your Cleopatra or Anthony in your arms is the most peaceful act a human being can perform. You can sing to Cleopatra, or quietly watch her sleep, or gaze into the eyes of the most precious gift that was given to you. **Look deeply** into your daughter's eyes. You will see pure, unconditional love for you, and you will see peace, devotion, and happiness in the depths of those eyes.

Rocking Chair

This rocking chair looks so quaint, one may think it gives the nursery a homey feeling. It may **look** great in the nursery, but I can attest (I had this one), that it is not comfortable! So, get your wife and yourself a very comfortable plush, rocker-recliner. It must be able to rock, not just recline. It may seem a bit costly, but this chair will be used for years. Perhaps a generous grandparent or local garage sale will make sure you have a rocking chair. The rocker-recliner is ESSENTIAL. The rocking motion grounds you and your child.

In the middle of the night, this chair will save your sanity, aching back, and tired body.

The rocking chair can be used for day or night feeding and cuddling when Cleopatra is a baby. Then as she grows, you will know the true purpose of this chair.

ROCKING CHAIR READER

Yes, the real reason for this chair is that you will be able to hold both Anthony and Cleopatra at the same time AND read to them.

Read all kinds of books! Read silly books, animal books, farm books, and rhyming books. Believe me, the books will magically appear, especially if you tell the grandparents to give them as gifts. But, if for any reason, there is a dry spell, the public library has a great selection of books. Hold Anthony on your lap and point to the pictures. Use your facial expressions to emphasize what is happening in the story.

Don't forget, your voice can also express the fun, the worry, and the simple banter that is in the story. This must be done every day until they are teenagers. And if you are lucky, they will love to have you read to them even then—just not in front of their friends.

Talk to Cleopatra

Tell her your adventures of the day—or maybe you can tell some great adventure story that you wish you had experienced, such as fishing in the quiet pond. Make sure you use descriptive words, like shallow, bottomless, murky, sparkling, clear, enormous, whopping, or miniscule. (Yes, girls like to fish, too.)

Perhaps you can tell her about the time you swung through the trees like Tarzan, or maybe about the time you were a great swashbuckling pirate out on the high seas, and you rescued the fair damsel in distress.

Or, what if the fair damsel rescued you? She also wants to hear about your trip to the post office, or the office mate who loves to pretend to work.

Your child needs words and lots of them. Use the kind of words you would use when speaking with your friends. <u>Do not oversimplify or speak in gibberish baby talk.</u>

You are creating the next great leader of the free world or at least the leader of her kindergarten class and your child will need an extensive vocabulary for that.

Stroller Rides and Fresh Air.

When Cleopatra is little, the stroller needs to protect her, but as she grows, you can use a stroller that is more open. In the beginning, if it is not too sunny, keep the top open so your little one can see the world all around her. Remember, EVERYTHING IS NEW to your baby.

Silly sounds are fascinating to your Anthony. When you become a father, your "coolness" factor changes. Anthony will be extremely impressed with whatever unusual sounds you can create with your mouth and hands.

Sudden sounds may scare him, but whistles and raspberries are rock music to his little ears.

Peek a Boo is a game that you can play with Cleopatra from a very young age. She really believes that you have disappeared when she can no longer see you.

Funny faces will never get old for her either. Believe it or not, her mother will get a laugh at your funny faces, too.

Grandparents

Grandparents want to give your child what they were not able to give you.   Again, it goes back to old expectations and the way they were parented.

Never stop a grandparent from giving your child a book. A book, read with expression and a cuddle, must be one of life's most priceless gifts. Therefore, a book is an ideal gift. Once the child has read the book several times, she will independently create her own stories from the pictures.

Now if you think grandparents look like the people in the above picture, think again. Most grandparents are active and will want to take your children on hikes (not major mountain climbing), trips and bike rides. Let the grandparents be as active with your children as possible. This may enlighten your father.

He will be so happy because he gets to do with your child what he wishes he would have done with you.

Be the enlightened one. Don't miss out!

Grandparents and Gifts

Now, the topic of grandparents and gifts. You can tell—oops, let me use the word *suggest*—that grandparents should not bring a gift every time they see their grandchild.

Your child just wants Grandma and Grandpa's attention. If the grandparents want to spend money and they are thinking of buying a gift that you are going to have to find space for after the child plays with it for a mere ten minutes, suggest that they put that money into a savings account that you have created for your child's college education.

Remember my comment about fiscal responsibility? Well, yes, college is something you need to think about. And, perhaps you can get the grandparents to contribute to it over the years and then college won't be such a burden.

They can open a "529 plan for Higher Education." This plan is exempt from federal taxes and can be used only for higher education expenses.

Or, for a plan with more flexible and less rigid rules they can invest in Savings Bonds or Mutual Funds. The grandparents will then feel they have given their grandchild a special gift that will keep on giving even after they are gone.

Box Creations

Use your imagination. A box can be anything you want it to be. Anthony will enjoy playing with objects that are not necessarily extraordinary, but often rather ordinary. A paper roll from toweling or toilet paper make great trumpets. Or, turn it into a rattle by filling it with dried beans or rice and tape it over the end with strong packing tape. Anthony will find fun in the box because your face lets him know he is using his imagination. He is looking for your approval. Let him be creative. Let him play with SAFE things like kettles and spoons (you will need earplugs quite often), and when you have had a tough day—plastic containers also work well and are easier on the headache.

When you play with Anthony and you come up with a great idea. Write it down—write it down here. You can use it again next month or with Cleopatra when she comes along.

Ideas

_____

_____

_____

_____

_____

_____

_____

Daddy-Time Tools

Toddler Time

WHAT ABOUT MY TIME?

There are days that you are so busy that you think you will never have time for yourself.

When you make unbreakable scheduled time for your child, you also have to make sure you **make time** for you and Mom. We are all busy. Yes, you will have to schedule time for yourself and dates, just like you do with the kids.

You are right, there is very little spontaneity with a family. You can be spontaneous when your children visit the grandparents for the weekend and when your children have left the house. Believe me, they will leave the house faster than you ever imagined.

Exercise is great for your mental health and increases your stamina to keep up with the kids. Exercise is easy to schedule. One of you can watch them while the other goes running or goes to the gym. Note: you must make sure your schedule allows for both of you to get your exercise.

MAKE A DATE! Go out to dinner or a movie. You need to keep your flame burning, too. You and your friends can exchange babysitting nights or days—a date does not have to be at night— and then you are not spending extra money on babysitting.

But the money spent on a babysitter is worth it. Here is a great idea for a birthday or holiday gift from grandparents. Ask for a movie theatre gift card and some cash for the babysitter. You will get more enjoyment out of that, than an ugly sweater!

No, you cannot spend the money on bills!

Toddler

Everything you did with Cleopatra as an infant is what you need to do with her as a small child.

So, hang onto the items in your tool box, and here are some items you will want to ADD to your box.

Most likely you will have received a book on nursery rhymes, but just in case, I've included a few popular rhymes in your Daddy Time Instruction Manual.   Read and recite nursery rhymes with your little one. Both Cleopatra and Anthony need to hear and recite these rhymes with you. If you have the book in front of you, show Cleopatra the pictures and point out what you are talking about.

I am sure you know most of these rhymes already, but if you don't, try to memorize two or three and then recite them while your daughter sits on your lap, lays in your arms or rides on your shoulders.

Some nursery rhymes can be sung.   Whenever you can move and gesture to the words, do so freely and flamboyantly!

Old King Cole

Old King Cole
Was a merry old soul
And a merry old soul was he;
He called for his pipe
And he called for his bowl
And he called for his fiddlers three
Every fiddler he had a fiddle
And a very fine fiddle had
he;
Oh, there's none so rare
As can compare
With King Cole and his fiddlers three.

One, Two, Three, Four

One, two, three, four, five,
Once I caught a fish alive,

Six, seven, eight, nine, ten,
Then I let it go again
Why did you let it go?

Because it bit my finger so.
Which finger did it bite?
This little finger on my right.

Diddle Diddle Dumpling, My Son John

Diddle Diddle Dumpling, my son John
Went to bed with his breeches on;
One stocking off, and one stocking on,
Diddle Diddle dumpling, my son John

The Grand Old Duke of York

Oh, the grand old Duke of York,
He had ten thousand men;
He marched them up to the top of the hill,
And he marched them down again.
And when they were up, they were up,
And when they were down, they were down,
And when they were only half way up,
They were neither up nor down

Lavender's blue

Lavender's blue, dilly dilly,
Lavender's green
When you are King, dilly dilly,
I shall be Queen
Who told you so, dilly dilly,
Who told you so?
'Twas my own heart, dilly dilly,
That told me so
Call up your friends, dilly, dilly
Set them to work
Some to the plough, dilly dilly,
Some to the fork
Some to the hay, dilly dilly,
Some to thresh corn
Whilst you and I, dilly dilly,
Keep ourselves warm
Lavender's blue, dilly dilly,
Lavender's green
When you are King, dilly dilly,
I shall be Queen
Who told you so, dilly dilly,
Who told you so?
'Twas my own heart, dilly dilly,
That told me so.

Humpty Dumpty

Humpty Dumpty sat on a wall;
Humpty Dumpty had a great fall.
All the King's horses
And all the King's men
Couldn't put Humpty together again!

Mulberry Bush

Here we go round the mulberry bush,
The mulberry bush, the mulberry bush,
Here we go round the mulberry bush,
On a cold and frosty morning.

This is the way we wash our hands,
Wash our hands, wash our hands,
This is the way we wash our hands,
On a cold and frosty morning.

This is the way we wash our clothes,
Wash our clothes, wash our clothes,
This is the way we wash our clothes,
On a cold and frosty morning.

This is the way we go to school,
Go to school, go to school,
This is the way we go to school,
On a cold and frosty morning.

This is the way we come out of school,
Come out of school, come out of school,
This is the way we come out of school,
On a cold and frosty morning.

Saw a Ship a-Sailing

I saw a ship a-sailing,
A-sailing on the sea;
And, oh! it was all laden
With pretty, things for thee!

There were comfits in the cabin,
And apples in the hold;
The sails were made of silk,
And the masts were made of gold.

The four-and-twenty sailors
That stood between the decks,

Were four-and-twenty white mice
With chains about their necks.

The captain was a duck,

With a packet on his back;
And when the ship began to move,
The captain said,

"Quack! Quack!"
"Quack! Quack!"
"Quack! Quack!"

I'm a Little Teapot

I'm a little teapot,
Short and stout!
Here is my handle;
Here is my spout.
When I get steamed up,
Hear me shout!
Just tip me over
And pour me out!

Jack and Jill

Jack and Jill went up the hill,
To fetch a pail of water;
Jack fell down and
broke his crown,
And Jill came tumbling after.

Then up Jack got and
off did trot,
As fast as he could caper,
To old Dame Dob,
who patched his nob
With vinegar and brown paper.

Jack Sprat

Jack Sprat could eat no fat,
His wife could eat no lean,
And so betwixt them both, you see,
They licked the platter clean.

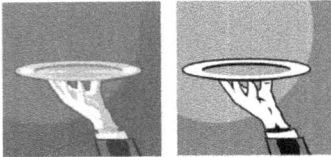

Cuddle

Cuddling is what you do on cold winter days or cool spring nights. Cleopatra or Anthony will love to sit next to you, especially with your arm around them.

You can do a variety of things while cuddling. You can do nothing more than sit quietly and swing on the porch swing. Or, you can watch the squirrels run across the squirrel highway (i.e. electric wires), high above the bushes and interspersed in the trees.

Or, you can check out the birds while you are sitting on your porch or in the backyard. Birds are as fascinating for your children as they are for you.

When it is too cold to be outside, watch the rain or the snow through a big window.

And, the best way to cuddle is with a good book!

Read, Read, Read, and Read Some More!

Cleopatra or Anthony will love reading because you will have read so many books to them. If by some strange happenstance you do not have any books in the house, remember, the public library has an unbelievable collection that is always accessible.

When you read, make sure the stories come to life by using your best and most expressive voice. Expression makes the stories sound exciting or scary or silly.

If you want to use voices, you can, however, if you simply read with feeling your child will develop a love of reading. You will be giving Cleopatra and Anthony a huge repertoire of vocabulary that will help them all through their schooling.

Vocabulary is developed by the language we encounter. We come across a greater vocabulary while reading than while merely speaking. When you are reading to your toddlers, point out characters, action, traits, facial features, and objects of interest.

Then, ask them questions about what is in the book. You can ask about colors and have them name the animals or items in the pictures. As they get older, ask them what happened in the book.

DIVERSIONS AND DELIGHTS

PLAY

There are so many ways to play with your child. Hide and Seek. Walking in the Park. Giving rides on your shoulders and laughing.

More Fun and Games

If you live in the cold, kids love to play in the snow. If you don't, they would love a snow adventure—especially if it is just you and Anthony or you and Cleopatra.

Dancing with Cleopatra will make her swoon. Letting her dance on your feet is so much fun. She will remember this, even on her wedding day.

Cook something creative or make simple sandwiches together.

Cooking is more problem solving. You need to decide what to eat, where to find it and what is a good recipe.

These are great lessons for life through fun!

FUN AND FROLIC

All you need is a strong back and lots of energy. Oh, don't be surprised if you walk into a few walls when you play hide and seek with a blindfold. It is all a part of being a Daddy

GAMES AND SPORTS

Your child <u>may</u> want to play team sports.

A little batting practice or one on one time on the court makes your child happy and feel special that Dad is taking time to be with them.

Perhaps sports came very easily to you, Dad, but Anthony might not like sports. There is nothing wrong with that!

It is all about having a good time with Daddy!

Magnetic Letters on the Refrigerator

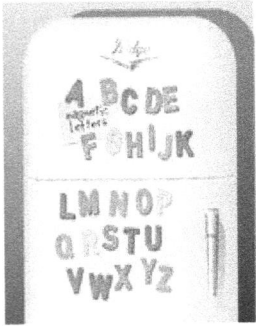

These magnetic letters should be included in your tool box as well as a little alphabet book to go along with them.

Please wait to start using these letters until your little one stops putting every little item into her mouth. In order for your little Cleopatra or Anthony to learn to read independently, they need to know the sounds of the letters. Every time you pick a letter say the **sound first** and then say the name.

You want your child to recognize the letters out of sequence, so place the letters helter-skelter on the refrigerator and ask Cleopatra or Anthony the sound of the letter and then the name.

If they don't get it right, DON'T SAY NO, just repeat the sound of the letter and the name. Repetition is the way we learn.

Write your child's name on the refrigerator and show it to her daily. You want your child to recognize his or her name immediately. By the time Anthony is four he must know his **last** name. If Cleopatra sees it and reads it daily- (this is a quick 10 second game) school will be a breeze. Don't forget, Grandma and Grandpa would love to have the little one recognize their names, too.

When your baby is small, these magnets need to be high on the refrigerator so she cannot choke on them accidently. (The new refrigerators don't hold magnets, so you may have to invest in a small magnetic board. Think garage sales.) When she grows a little, you can start putting the letters at her level and she can begin to manipulate them.

When the letters are at her level, you need to be there with her. This is not a game to keep her busy. This is an interactive game with Daddy.

Puzzles

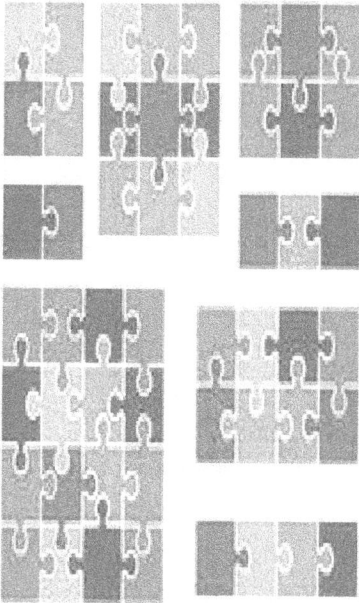

Other items that may be included in your tool box are puzzles. Again, these are <u>not</u> to be set out for Cleopatra to play with by herself.

She will chew on them, spit on them, and totally reshape them into something that will not fit together as a puzzle.

These puzzles are small enough that you can do them in one sitting—remember we are thinking toddler—not baby at this point. If your child does not have the attention to put it together, then this is a project that may have to wait until Cleopatra and Anthony are a little older. Remember toddlers are from two to four years—sometimes to age five. A few children even start younger—you have to read your child's ability and attention span.

When Cleopatra is old enough and she enjoys her puzzles, there may be days when she is distracted and cannot finish it. In order to make your time with her special, you may want to use a cutting board as the base for these small puzzles, so you can continue at a later time.

Do not get frustrated with your little one if she is distracted. Do not force her to finish the project. Come back to it in a little while or perhaps the next day.

Do not use your time as a punishment. Don't tell your child you won't play if they don't _____ (Fill in the blank.) I do not have to fill in the blank because there will be so many phrases that can go on that line that it would fill 100 volumes.

So Much About Puzzles

When you are puzzling with your little one, ask her to show you the top, bottom, sides and up and down of the puzzle.

Ask her which piece she put in BEFORE or AFTER the one you are working on. These placement words are essential for their learning.

Have Anthony talk about the shape. This has a groove—yes use the correct vocabulary. This one has the "tongue". You can also say the ying and the yang. When children recognize shapes and focus on the shapes, this will also help them with learning sight words. Words have shapes so let's point out the shapes early.

You can TOGETHER count the puzzle pieces. If one is missing, you have to find it. You may want to "hide" one to make sure they remember how many pieces there are. (This is NOT something you do with a 1000-piece puzzle!)

And that leads me to common sense.

Use your **_common sense_** and you will have fun with your little one.

Puppets

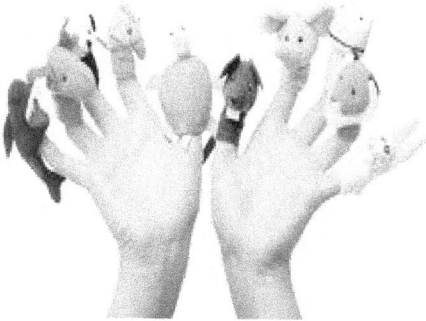

Finger Puppets

There is such a great variety in puppets. They can be simple, ornate, handmade or even purchased.

When you are playing with puppets, make sure you use your imagination, and this is the time you want to use voices.

Create stories and soon you will see your daughter using her imagination and telling her own stories.

Sock Puppets

We all know that the dryer eats socks. So, when you cannot find the match to one of your white socks, put it in your tool box.

You can use a permanent marker to draw a face on the sock and you have "Socksee" to play with "Dexxy." Dexxy is your index finger as a puppet—more to come on that.

Remember, your tool box does not need more than three socks, so once the dryer eats the fourth sock, you get to put it in your pile of single socks. You will note, I did not add socks to your tool box.

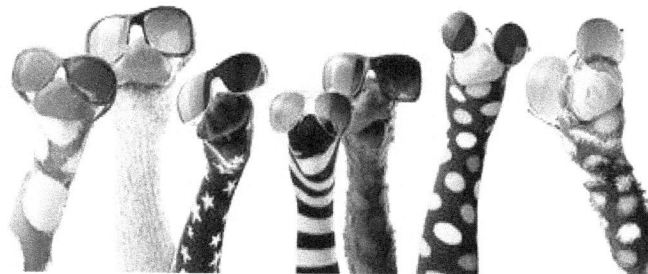

Hand Puppets

Hopefully, your tool box will include a hand puppet. It may be a cow, a hippo, a duck, or a frog, but whatever puppet you receive, your puppet will come alive once you give it a name.

The name can change depending on the whim of you or your child, or whatever traits your character must have in your story.

However, you cannot rely on the inanimate object to provide the complete entertainment for your Cleopatra. Again, you need to come up with stories. They can be very short, or long. It may merely be a conversation between Cleopatra and Dandelion.

Be mindful that some characters or puppets may frighten the child. Put it away until she is a little older.   You will see that there are some things your Cleopatra may love and others she hates.   Perhaps you will be surprised because Anthony might be just the opposite. Or, he could be exactly the same.

Your hand can be a very simple puppet, with two or three fingers painted.

Or, it can be a more sophisticated puppet in which you make a fist and your thumb becomes the mouth by moving up and down. The tip of the thumb needs to be touching the index finger.   The eyes of your character need to be put on either side of the index finger knuckle.

If you are in a situation where you do not have the ingredients for the paint, you can use a ball point pen to draw on your hand or even on your index finger. "Dexxy" can tell a lot of stories and keep Anthony occupied for quite a while.

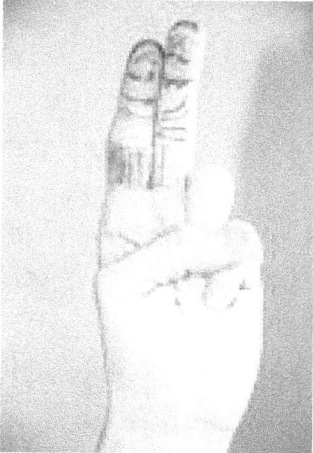

Painted Faces on Hands and Fingers

You are feeling creative and you want to paint a face on your hand. Or mom may want to paint it on your hand for you.

Where do you get the paint? You make it! It is easy to use and can be used to paint your hand or to do some face painting.

Recipe: Mix 2 Tablespoons cornstarch with 1 Tablespoon vegetable shortening, or you can substitute a skin sensitive lotion for the oil. Then add 3 drops of food coloring.

Your hand puppet can be made quickly with one color—or Dad, you can really use your imagination and create your own sweet character. A word to the wise, your child will remember what your puppet looked like. So, make sure you take a picture of it so you can re-create it.

Put a photo of your creations on the refrigerator and have your child talk about the character and what the character said. This is a great tool to use when you have some important lesson to teach because they will be focusing all their attention on this interesting character-- and you will be surprised how much your child will remember of what the "Hand Man" said but will forget what the "Man" (Dad) said.

This does not have to be a long drawn out puppet session. It can be done quickly before bedtime or dinner. Or maybe when you want Cleopatra to eat her Brussels sprouts. You can also make a bigger production—shoe boxes make a great stage and the kitchen table can be converted into a "back stage" in seconds.

Silly Songs

Don't be surprised that when you are riding in a car, no matter how long or short the ride is, Cleopatra or Anthony will get bored. Boredom leads to a cranky child which leads to a miserable ride. A miserable ride may be only 10 minutes, but believe me, it can feel like 10 hours. So, you will need a repertoire of silly songs.

Now, you need to introduce these songs when your child is not cranky, or the songs will not work their magic. You can sing these songs while YOU are giving them a bath. Bath time is great fun and songs are always sung out on the high seas.

Never, ever, ever, ever, ever, ever, ever, leave your child unattended in the tub. If the phone rings, let it ring. If someone is at the door, have them wait until you take Anthony <u>out of the tub</u>. Don't think that if you can hear him singing, everything is fine.

When you go on walks around the neighborhood, or while Anthony is swinging on the swings in the park, you can sing these songs. By the way, the parents around you will love you and I can guarantee they may smile, but secretly they are memorizing the words, so they can sing these same songs to their children.

There will be infinite opportunities to sing. Also, I have read that singing and humming helps clear up sinus problems. Hey, this is easy research and the remedy is free—so go for it. SING!

In an earlier section of your instruction manual it mentions playing your guitar. Please check the internet for the music to these songs. If your beautiful wife plays the piano, or the Kazoo, she can accompany you and Anthony. Just playing the melody makes it even more special for your child.

A family that sings together, stays **sane** together.

Silly Songs

Here are just a few songs for you to memorize. Once you start singing, I am sure you will remember your mother or grandparents singing these songs. Oh, and again, these simple verses will help them in school.   You are providing vocabulary for them

Bringing Home A Baby Bumble Bee

I'm bringing home a baby bumblebee,
Won't my mommy be so proud of me,
I'm bringing home a baby bumblebee,
Won't my mommy be so proud of me!
Ouch! It stung me! (Spoken)

I'm squishing up the baby bumblebee,
Won't my mommy be so proud of me,
I'm squishing up the baby bumblebee,
Won't my mommy be so proud of me!
Ooh! It's yucky! (Spoken)

I'm wiping off the baby bumblebee,
Won't my mommy be so proud of me,
I'm wiping off the baby bumblebee,
Now my mommy won't be mad at me!

Where Oh Where Has My Little Dog Gone

Oh, where, oh, where has my little dog gone?
Oh, where, oh, where can he be?
With his ears cut short and his tail cut long,
Oh, where, oh, where can he be?

London Bridge is Falling Down

London Bridge is falling down,
Falling down, falling down.
London Bridge is falling down,
My fair lady.

Take a key and lock her up
Lock her up, lock her up.
Take a key and lock her up.
My fair lady.

How will we build it up,
Build it up, build it up?
How will we build it up,
My fair lady.

Build it up with silver and gold,
Silver and gold, silver and gold.
Build it up with silver and gold,
My fair lady.

Gold and silver I have none,
I have none, I have none.
Gold and silver I have none,
My fair lady.

Build it up with needles and pins,
Build it up with needles and pins
Build it up with needles and pins,
My fair lady.

Pins and needles bend and break,
Bend and break, bend and break.
Pins and needles bend and break,
My fair lady.

Build it up with wood and clay,
Wood and clay, wood and clay.
Build it up with wood and clay,
My fair lady.

Wood and clay will wash away,
Wash away, wash away.
Wood and clay will wash away,
My fair lady

Build it up with stone so strong,
Stone so strong, stone so strong.
Build it up with stone so strong,
My fair lady.

Stone so strong will last so long,
Last so long, last so long.
Stone so strong will last so long,
My fair lady

Muffin Man

Do you know the Muffin Man?
The Muffin Man,
The Muffin Man,
Do you know the Muffin Man
Who lives in Drury Lane?

Yes, I know the Muffin Man,
The Muffin Man,
The Muffin Man.
Yes, I know the Muffin Man
Who lives in Drury Lane

Rain, Rain Go Away

Rain, rain, go away,
Come again another day;
Little *Anthony wants to play.

Rain, rain, go away,
Come again another day.
Rain, rain, go to Spain.
Never show your face again.

*(Fill in either Cleopatra's or Anthony's name)

The Simple Things

There will always be an endless supply of chores for you to do, but Cleopatra's time as a toddler or a child is very short, and it does have an end!   Therefore, from the simple to the silly to the mundane, these are the things that you will enjoy this short time.

Feed the birds.

Open your door and head to the back yard and the bird feeder. Once you are back inside and you are holding your child, gaze out the window and show Cleopatra the beauty of the birds.

fill

If you know the names of the birds, tell her because she needs vocabulary. You can also make a quick trip to the park and feed the ducks by the pond. DO NOT FEED THEM BREAD! Feed them corn, (canned, frozen, or fresh), peas, lettuce, oats or bird seeds.

Smell the flowers.

As you stroll down the street or play in the park, stop and smell the flowers. Make sure Cleopatra or Anthony don't pick the flowers. **Teach them to enjoy the beauty in simple things and to leave them grow for others to enjoy.**

This is something that you **need to teach** them. Your children will be bombarded with so much from the various forms of media.

Please take the TIME and show them how to appreciate simple beauty and simple things.

Splash in the Puddles!
Just make sure Mom doesn't find out you started it!

When Daddy acts silly in the rain, believe me, Cleopatra will hang onto this very special memory for a lifetime.

However, you must explain that only on very special occasions may she step in the puddles. Those special occasions are when YOU are there to make sure it is safe. Which means you are hanging onto her hand.

If she splashes when you are not around, she will not be able to slosh in the rain.

So, to play this game, and to assure that no one catches a cold, just grab a couple of those single socks that you are keeping in your tool box and use them to dry off the shoes and pant legs of Cleopatra. It also hides the evidence from Mom—just as long as you do the laundry.

COLORING AND PAINTING

There is an artist in all of us and your children are no exception. However, for them to be artists, we must cultivate their abilities and interests.

Start out simple. It makes no difference if you can only draw a stick figure—just remember, your drawing will be better than that of a toddler.

Find inexpensive newsprint and let Anthony scribble scrabble over the whole page, or if he wants, let him just put a small line on the page. It is his art—not yours.

Another idea is to use butcher paper and tape it to a child's table. Both Cleopatra and Anthony can color all over it and you just need to change it once a week.

Inexpensive coloring books are a lot of fun, but not necessary. You can draw circles and squares and have Anthony color those. Do NOT stress if Anthony cannot color within the lines. Give him time. His fine motor skills take time to develop and remember, sometimes it is better to think/color outside the box.

Water colors and a simple paintbrush will bring out the artist in everyone. Do not give Cleopatra a coloring book and tell her to color or place her in front of an easel and expect her to paint while you are busy doing something else. You need to be sitting with her and talking about the day, the weather and/or about the art.

Anthony wants and NEEDS your attention!

He does not want to be kept busy while you relax.

Homemade Projects

I will conclude this section with ideas for some home "cooked" creations.

You can call them chemistry projects.

Homemade Glue Projects

There will be rainy days when you both want to create something with your hands. Again, we need to think about the fact that Anthony may want to put everything into his mouth. Therefore, we want to play with a safe glue.

Homemade glue is not toxic because it is made of flour and water. Kids love to glue just about anything. I suggest you find inexpensive things to make their creations out of. Newsprint is great for gluing and creating. You can make paper sculptures; cover them with the glue and then paint.

Here is the **recipe for a homemade glue.**

This glue will last for months if you **keep it in the refrigerator**. If Anthony is interested, let him watch you. If he is only interested in the hot water, make the glue while he is napping and then take it out for him to play later.

1/2 cup flour
3 cups boiling water
3/4 cup cold water

Measure the flour into an unbreakable bowl and then slowly pour cold <u>water</u> into the flour and stir to form a paste. Carefully drop the paste into the boiling water, stirring constantly with a wire whip. Cook it over low heat for 5 minutes or until it thickens into a soft pliable glue. Once your concoction has cooled, pour it into a plastic squeeze bottle. Be sure to label it glue, so Mom doesn't use it in tomorrow's dinner. Remember, keep this in the refrigerator.

HOME-MADE CLAY

When you play with home-made clay, let Cleopatra use her imagination to create new timeless masterpieces. You also are giving her a chance to strengthen her fingers and improve her fine motor ability. This is your chance to let her show **you** what she can make.

Always ask what she has made! She will stop creating if you do not know what it is. DO NOT BE A CRITIC! It may look like a horse in her mind—even though no one else sees it. But that is ok. Do not discourage her.

Home-Made Clay Recipe

4 cups water
4 tablespoons oil
4 cups flour
1/2 cup cream of tartar
1 cup salt

Mix all ingredients together in a sauce pan. Cook and stir over low heat until the Home-made Clay is completely formed and is not sticky. At this point add several drops of food coloring. Or, if you want several more colors, divide the mixture into balls and add different colors to each ball. Make sure you let it cool a bit. Then, store it in an air tight container or a re-closable plastic bag.

GUCK MUCK

1 1/3 cups warm water
1 cup water
4 teaspoons Borax
1 cup white glue
6 drops food coloring

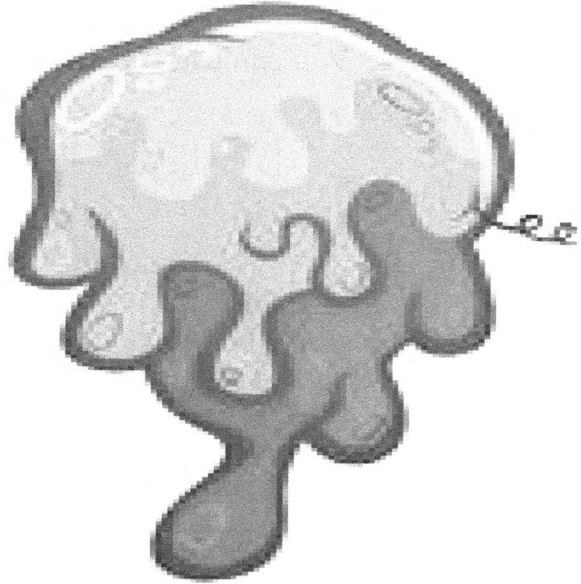

In one bowl, mix 1 cup white glue, 1 cup water and 6 drops food coloring.   In a separate bowl dissolve 4 teaspoons Borax in 1 1/3 cups warm water.

Once the Borax is dissolved, add the Borax brew to the glue mixture and squeeze it into muck.

It doesn't stay in any one shape for long, but it certainly is fun to play with. Anthony will love the Guck Muck!

When you play with Cleopatra and you come up with a great idea. Write it down here. You can use it again next month or with Anthony when he comes along.

Ideas:

_____

_____

_____

_____

_____

_____

_____

_____

_____

_____

_____

_____

_____

_____

Daddy-Time Tools

Child Time

THE CHILD

All too soon you will find little Cleopatra or Anthony heading to elementary school.

Both Cleopatra and Anthony REALLY need your TIME, particularly at this point in their lives.

What can you do with your little one when they are of school age?   You can continue to do all the fun things that you did with them as toddlers. In this section, a few more things will be added to your repertoire with your school-aged child.

Reading with them will always be of the utmost importance.

LISTEN!
LISTEN!
LISTEN!

Cleopatra may be telling you all about her day in full detail. But while Anthony is telling you about his day you may note that he only talks about certain things. You need to listen to what he is <u>leaving out</u> of the conversation.

Anthony may not be able to tell you what is bothering him. If he talks about all aspects of school, except his friends, then it is essential to ask him about his friends, because it <u>may</u> mean that he is having friend issues. If he cannot tell you what he is learning, you need to ask about it.

This is not gender specific! Your son may tell you everything and your daughter will leave things out.

No matter what, ask them both what they **learned** in school, *not* what they <u>*did*</u> during the day. **Don't settle for "nothing"!**

You need to ask specific questions to help them learn how to tell you what they learned. It is important to be consistent and do this every day. Let them know that this will be your question every day, so they will be prepared with an answer.

If Anthony can tell you what he learned, you are reinforcing his learning in a comfortable, conversational way. Maybe, let Cleopatra's teacher know you are asking this question and she will do a quick review at the end of class. (The other parents will appreciate this, too.)

ROSE, THORN, BUD

Conversations are very important, particularly at dinner. (Never go by the adage that children should be seen and not heard. If you don't hear them, you won't be able to correct their misconceptions or hear their concerns. One conversation starter that I learned from a lovely, southern, woman, Paige Hahn, is called "Rose, Thorn, Bud".

Ask Cleopatra or Anthony to tell you what the "**<u>rose</u>**" of the day was for them. Rose means the best part of the day, the most fun, the most exciting, the most intriguing thing that they did.

Ask what the "thorn" of the day was. What made them mad, sad, angry, frustrated, or disappointed. This is any part of their day that they didn't like, not just at school.

Finally, ask them what the "bud" of the day was. The bud is what they are looking forward to, such as a trip to the park on the weekend, the grandparents visiting, a camping trip, or pizza movie night. It can be anything that is important to them—even if you don't like it—listen to what is important to them.

The order does not have significance! Sometimes Anthony comes home upset about something. All he can think about is the thorn or the thorns of his day. Let him start with the thorn, let him talk it out. Give him some time and then ask what their bud is –to ease away from the negative thoughts.

Mom and Dad also need to state their Rose, Thorn, and Bud as well. Dad may start with a rose and doesn't get to finish because Cleopatra must tell the "rose" that she is so excited about. But, go back and finish. Let them know what your thorn was and to what you are looking forward. Too often kids don't think parents have thorns.

If it was a particularly bad day, you may have to suggest a rose for Cleopatra. It could be a good friend, or that their pet sat next them because he knew she was sad, just so they will learn to appreciate the small, wonderful things that we often take for granted.

CLOUDS,
DINOSAURS, DRAGONS AND ANGELS

Clouds are a constant resource for child's infinite imagination.

Lay on the ground or sit in a comfortable chair that allows you to sky gaze. You can also cloud gander in a car, but make sure the driver has his/her eyes on the road, not in the clouds!

Observe the white, fluffy clouds rolling by—or even the feathery wisps that float across the sky.

Each cloud is unique. As you peer at each cloud, what does the cloud look like? Don't say "a cloud." What sort of item or animal does it remind Anthony of? What does it remind you of? Who does it remind you of? Could it be Aunt Mable or Uncle Theodore?

Is it a sea serpent? Dragon? Angel? Teddy Bear? Fish? Cow? Tree?

A flying alligator eating a witch's cauldron?

Of course, it won't look exactly like what your child says it is, but somehow the shape gives Cleopatra a sense of what it is. So, go with it!

Decorate an Ornament for A Summer Tree

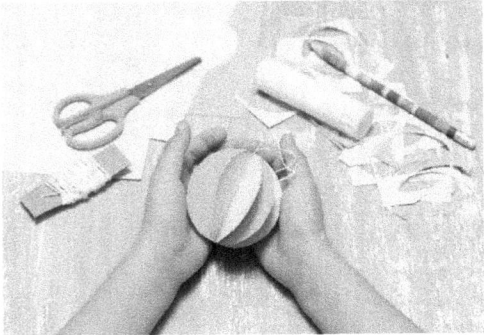

Create an ornament out of a balloon, newspaper and glue, using the glue recipe you used when Cleopatra was a toddler. Or, you can simply cut them out of paper.

Next, paint or color your ornament and add decorations for a particular time of year. Since this is Daddy-Time, you can create a "Summer tree" or a "School Tree." Another idea is to create an ornament for every summer based on what you did or where you traveled. A Summer Tree can be branches and twigs of various sizes placed in a vase or a pot.

Also, at the end of each year, you may want to put a picture on an ornament of what Cleopatra felt was the most important thing she learned or did that year.

As a variation on those ornaments, you can decorate mini clay pots and then use a lanyard or yarn to hang them.

You can create your own tradition of giving a homemade ornament to Mom each Christmas, Eid or Hanukah.

Then, with great ceremony, place the ornament on whatever tree you create, either the summer tree, the school tree, or the holiday tree. I can guarantee that Anthony will cherish and long remember the time he spent making them with you.

COLLEGE

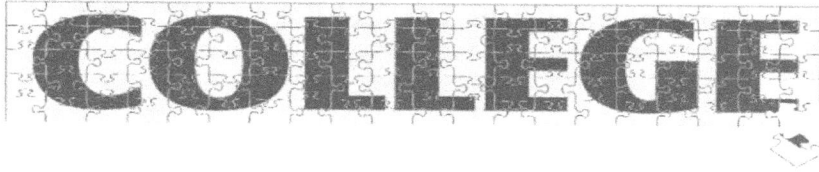

TALK ABOUT COLLEGE

You may be questioning if I erroneously put this page in the wrong section. This section of the book is for elementary aged children!

No, it _is_ in the right section.

When you talk to your 6-10-year-old about college, do not mention that they will be moving out. At this age, your child fears being separated from you. If they are worried, tell them they can stay with you. At this stage they need to feel your constant presence.

However, for your teenager, the thought of moving out is a great incentive for them to go to college.

College or a Post High School Technical School must be Anthony and Cleopatra's trajectory through school.

It is never too early to talk about college with your children!

Start with simple non-threatening references to college.

_Cleopatra may ask a question that will need a quick check on the internet. Once you find the answer and she is excited about it, simply state that _____ might be something she would like to study in college. Then leave it at that._

Both Anthony and Cleopatra will have lots of questions and slowly you will make college a part of their mindset.

College doesn't have to be a 4-year program. If Cleopatra likes to take apart and fix things, a technical school may be the answer.

YES, COLLEGE BEGINS IN KINDERGARTEN!

Your school principal may have already told you that what your child learns in Kindergarten will be carried through college. Kindergarten is the foundation for all learning.

This is absolutely my best work.
I tried my hardest.
Be proud of me

Do not demand perfect grades. Let them focus on learning and enjoying learning.

Be involved in your child's elementary, middle, and high school!

If Cleopatra is trying her hardest and doing her best, that is perfect for elementary school. (Just don't tell your children, as this is information for your eyes only.) In order for kids to stay in school longer, they need to like going to school and look at school as a positive experience. School is not always fun, but it should be a positive experience.

If you get upset because you know <u>you</u> would have done better, you are not helping Anthony. **Anthony is not you**. He may do better or worse than you did, but your job is to constantly encourage him in positive ways.

The grades that are important for college are the grades your child earns in 10th-12th grade. Do not tell your child this, but you will be less stressed and more focused on your children learning the concepts and content. If they know those, they will get good grades in high school.

Don't get me wrong, it is important to have high expectations for your child. You and your child both need high expectations but putting pressure on them for certain grades in elementary school can be detrimental. Once they start to hate school and hate the stress, it is very difficult to get them back on track.

Planting Seeds

Anthony and Cleopatra will love to plant seeds with you and watch them grow. They both will ask lots of questions. Some questions you will know the answer to, and some you will not.

Now, <u>you</u> may love gardening, but that does not mean your child wants to help with all facets of gardening.   The fact that your child loves planting seeds in a few paper cups or clay pots does not mean he will be a gardener.

When you do plant your garden, give your child a specific job, such as putting the seeds in the already prepared holes. Do not tell them to plant the seeds while you do something else. I can guarantee that is a recipe for disaster.

Weeding is a part of gardening, but not something I suggest you have your young child attempt. Anthony cannot distinguish between a plant and a weed. You will get frustrated and then the whole idea of being together with dad, just went down the tube. Remember, the time you spend with your child, Daddy, is the most important thing you can do in your adult life.

Plant the seeds in a flower box, or flower pots. You can watch them grow and then give them to Mom as a gift, or they can be replanted outside. Once you do that, it's now your responsibility to find new kinds of seeds to plant. Anthony may discover a new vegetable that he likes and will eat for the rest of his life because he planted it with dad.

What about purple cauliflower, purple carrots or purple Brussels sprout?

Conquer the Squirrels

Squirrels are hungry and very persistent. If that bird seed is hanging out on that tree, squirrels will do all in their power to get it.   Life is a series of problems—some small and some not so small.

Problem solving is what your children will need to do daily. Talk to them about how you plan to solve the squirrel problem. How are you going to prevent the squirrel from eating all the seeds?

Let your children hear your thinking process so when they come across a problem, the time you spent with them will not only be fun, but it will be the help that they need to solve their future problems. Speak out loud what you are thinking. Model problem solving. This is a perfect time for you to talk to yourself, just don't mumble.

As an example, you can say, "What would happen if we put a cover over the bird feeder? Then you discuss out loud why it would work and why it wouldn't work. Talk about how you would cover it by continuing to talk to yourself, "I have a can that I could hang over it, but the problem with that, is that the squirrels won't get to it, but the birds won't get to it either."

Let them know that you don't come up with the right answer the first time you think about the problem.   Let them know that answers don't magically pop into your head and then suddenly you have the answers.

If you teach them problem solving, then school problem solving will be much easier for them. This is another way you are preparing them for college. But most of all, you are having fun with your children.

Oh, and one suggestion to help conquer the squirrel. Try greasing the pole that the feeder is on with vegetable shortening. The slippery pole should stop those marauders from clawing up to the yummy bird feed. Voila, dad has solved the problem—oh and Cleopatra will have so much fun smearing shortening up and down that pole.

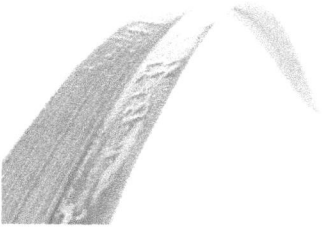

Whistle with a Blade of Grass

Hold a wide, flat, piece of grass between your thumbs. The blade of grass should be as long as your thumbs. Place the blade so it is centered between the thumbs and then blow through your thumbs.

This creates a very special whistle.   It is free and there is an endless supply of blades of grass. Experts suggest you use course grass as it creates a better whistle. An interesting fact is that *this music maker is not a whistle, it is a reed instrument.*

Remind Anthony, Cleopatra, and yourself, that it takes practice to learn how to do this. But. if everyone keeps practicing that blade of grass will whistle.

Once they are successful at this, it will give them confidence to try something else.

Your children need to feel confident based on their effort and successes, not merely based on your words or opinions.

NOTES IN THEIR LUNCH BOX OR SNACK BAG

Surprise Cleopatra with fun facts or weird laws!

Your child wants to know that you are thinking about them. We are all busy, but if you put a few words on a card it will be something that you two can share.

Sometimes, kids think they are too old for a simple "I love you" note, but if you write a few "fun facts" or "weird laws" on a sheet of paper, it will be a conversation starter for your child.

If your child is shy, this can help them make friends.

You can write several "notes" for the week, and these notes will lead to great dinner conversations with the family. Anthony will have a great lunch in two ways. He'll have good food, and all his classmates will want to sit with him to find out the weird law or fun fact that you sent that day.

A few examples of weird laws are:

No one may wash a mule on the sidewalk in Culpepper, Virginia.

Spitting on seagulls is not allowed in Norfolk, Virginia.

No one may have a skunk as a pet in Prince William County, Virginia

Surprisingly, in Tennessee, it is against the law to drive a car while sleeping.

A 1925, a California law says it is illegal to wiggle while dancing.

It's law that a person must take a bath at least once a year! At least in Kentucky it is!

In Phoenix, Arizona, a person may not walk through a hotel lobby with his spurs on.

In Kansas, you cannot drive a buffalo through the streets.

Weird State Laws

DID YOU KNOW? A HIPPO CAN FIT A 4-FOOT-TALL CHILD IN ITS OPEN MOUTH.

In Alaska, it is illegal to wake a sleeping bear to take a picture.

It is illegal to wear a fake mustache that causes laughter in church, in Alabama.

Arizona established that it is illegal for donkeys to sleep in a bathtub.

California decreed that a frog that dies during a frog-jumping contest, cannot be legally eaten.

A pickle cannot be legally considered a pickle unless it bounces, according to Connecticut law.

Georgia established that it is illegal to keep an ice cream cone in your back pocket on Sunday.

Idaho voted in that it is illegal to give your sweetheart a box of chocolate that weighs more than 50 pounds.

Indiana passed a law that mustaches are illegal if the bearer has the tendency to habitually kiss other human beings.

Iowa dictated, that one-armed piano players, must by law, perform for free.

Michigan men proclaimed that it is illegal for a woman to cut her own hair without her husband's permission.

Minnesota made into law that a duck may not cross state lines with another duck on top of his/her head. Yes, I said duck!

More Weird Laws

Cattle or any livestock CANNOT ride on a school bus in Florida.

It is illegal for camels to run without a leash or rope in the streets of Galveston, Texas.

North Dakota considers it illegal to lie down and fall asleep with your shoes on!

Ohio constituted a law that it is illegal to get a fish drunk!

In Vermont men wrote a law stating that women must get written permission from their husbands to wear false teeth.

In Wyoming, it was voted in that one may not take a picture of a rabbit from January to April without official permission

In Virginia, chickens have scheduled working hours. Chickens cannot lay their eggs before 8 a.m. and they must be finished laying them by 4 p.m.

In Colorado, pet cats, like cars, MUST have a tail light, if they are running loose outside.

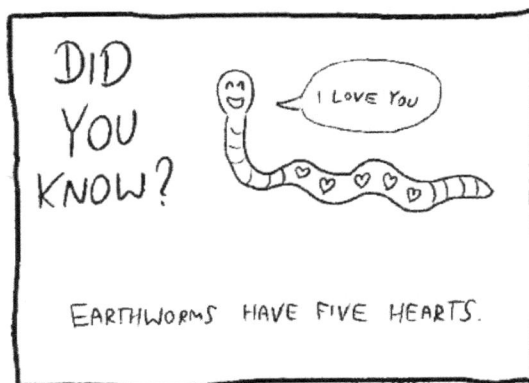

DID YOU KNOW?

I LOVE YOU

EARTHWORMS HAVE FIVE HEARTS.

I'M NOT MAKING THESE LAWS UP!

Missouri ratified that it is illegal to drive with an uncaged bear.

Nevada put through a law making it illegal to drive a camel on the highway.

New Jersey men decreed that it is illegal for a man to knit during the fishing season.

DID YOU KNOW?

GIRAFFE HAS SUCH A LONG TONGUE IT CAN LICK ITS EARS.

New York put in force that slippers cannot be worn after 10 p.m.

California law ordered that there cannot be any more than 3000 sheep being herded down Hollywood Blvd, at one time.

It was determined in West Virginia that no children can attend school with their breath smelling of wild onions.

Finally, this is a great way to curb any kind of inappropriate language.

West Virginia ratified that for each act of public swearing, a person will be fined one dollar. (When your Cleopatra is a teenager, you will either never have to pay an allowance, or you will make a fortune.)

Don't forget, this applies to you, too.

Both Anthony and Cleopatra should try to come up with weird laws and facts. It will lead to a great discussion of how the laws came about and a little bit about geography.

Again, it is problem solving—someone saw a problem and wondered how to solve it. The best part of this silliness is that you are interacting with your child.

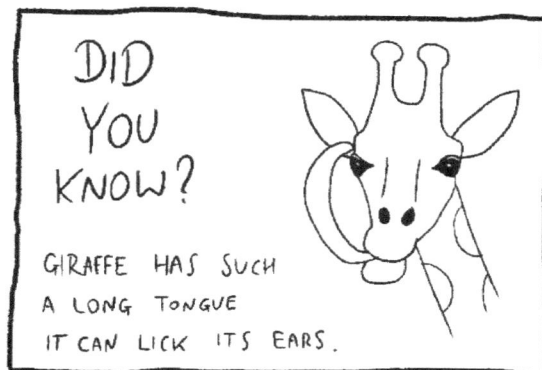

Puzzles

If Cleopatra and Anthony enjoyed puzzles as a toddler, they will continue to enjoy them with you. The puzzles, now, can be a little bigger. Take a cardboard box and cut it so the puzzle will fit on it easily. Then, no matter where you put it together, you can easily move it, so it is not in the way. You can also use a card table to hold your masterpiece. When you put the larger puzzles together, take a few minutes each day to place a few pieces. Do not force them. If they don't feel like it, you work a little on it and they may change their mind or learn from you that you are being persistent in your finding solutions for difficult problems. When they do work on it, this is your time to listen to Cleopatra and Anthony. Kids say a lot when they are not talking to you directly, but if they are doing something else—like playing or puzzling—they may share a lot with you. And, these are the things you need to hear.

Face Painting

Use the same recipe that you used for painting on your hand. Mix 2 Tablespoons cornstarch with 1 Tablespoon vegetable shortening and add 3 drops of food coloring. Use a different container for each color. Then, you can paint butterflies on your daughter and turn both your children into an action hero. It doesn't matter if you are very artistic or not, your children will love the special time and effort that Daddy made for them. You may have a line of children waiting to have their faces painted on lazy summer days or at his/her birthday party. Be prepared!

Kid Appropriate Jokes

Memorize some kid appropriate jokes and then share them with your children. You do not have to be a great comedian, yet your children will love laughing with you.

Check the internet for some kid appropriate jokes. Or, you can find a book with kid's jokes and memorize them. (Ask a Grandparent to supply a book or visit the public library.) You may think the jokes are ridiculous, but your kids will laugh heartily at them.

Most importantly, they will love you for the jokes, because you are spending time with them. Memorizing will also keep YOUR brain healthy.

Memorize Home Address and Telephone Number.

This is a game that you <u>must</u> play with Cleopatra and Anthony. Please make sure they memorize their address and a telephone number by first grade, **and** each time you move. Turn these memorizing tasks into games. See who can memorize the fastest. (Note to dad—let them memorize faster than you can.)

Give them tools on memorizing, such as linking the address or phone number to a song, chunking the number (a phone number is already chunked for you) or repeating and walking. The movement of the body helps them memorize, too.

Volunteer!

Volunteer in Their Classrooms

Anthony will be so proud to see you in his classroom. Don't be shy. When I was principal, there were a lot of men who volunteered in classrooms. Let me assure you that your child will beam when his/her Daddy is giving his time for them and their learning.

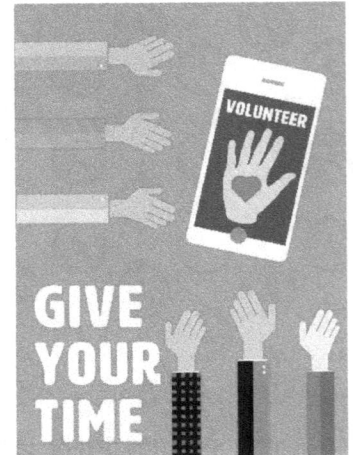

Volunteer to Coach **Whatever** Sport They Enjoy.

If you enjoy and understand a team sport, Cleopatra would love to have you as a coach. If you know nothing about the game except when to shout because your daughter made a goal, then perhaps you better settle for making sure you attend ALL her games. It is not enough that mom goes to the games, she needs to see dad at the games. You may be busy, but remember, you cannot be too busy to give your child your time. I've met too many men who regret not going to their children's games.

Volunteer to be Part of Scouts

Scouting or 4-H is very much like coaching a sport. You may not have grown up with scouting, so being a scout leader may not be your thing. However, make sure you attend Anthony's scout and 4-H meetings.

Take Them Fishing.

You do **not** need to buy an expensive fishing rod—a stick with a string attached is a great place to start.

If you spend a lot of money on equipment and then you find your child is not into fishing, it is a waste of money, which leads to anger and frustration on your part that you spent so much money and your child doesn't even like it!

So, start simple. And sometimes, the simplest toys are the best. And these are the ones they remember the most.

Don 't forget they will imitate you. If you are only willing to use the top of the line equipment—guess what they are going to want? And remember, you are paying for it.

FISHING LICENSE

Make sure you get a license to fish!

A stick with a string NEEDS a license.

People have found out the hard way that no matter the equipment, you still need the license.

Spend TIME going to their soccer, basketball, baseball, and water polo games and cheer loudly for them!!!!

By this time, you will have accumulated some great ideas, too.

But we all know, if we do not write them down, they are lost. So, when you play with Anthony, and you come up with a great idea, write it down—write it down here. You can use the idea again next month or with Cleopatra when she comes along.

Ideas:

_____

_____

_____

_____

_____

_____

_____

_____

_____

_____

_____

_____

_____

The Clock is Ticking!

YOU HAVE ONLY A FEW MORE YEARS

TO MAKE A DIFFERENCE

You may be afraid to turn the page because you have heard so many horror stories about the teenage years.

You have about 16 years to make a difference in the life of your child. And, that may be pushing it. It may only be 12 years.

Peers start playing a huge role and they have an even bigger effect on your children.

There is always hope if you spend time with them.

Dad-Time Tools
Teenager Time

Good Luck!

Bona Fortuna!

Viel Gluck!

Guid Luck!

Boa Sorte!

Bon Suerte!

Bon Chans!

Bon Chance!

Suette!

Buena Suete!

Bona Sort!

Stretno!

Hazz Sa-eed!

Amoor Zoo!

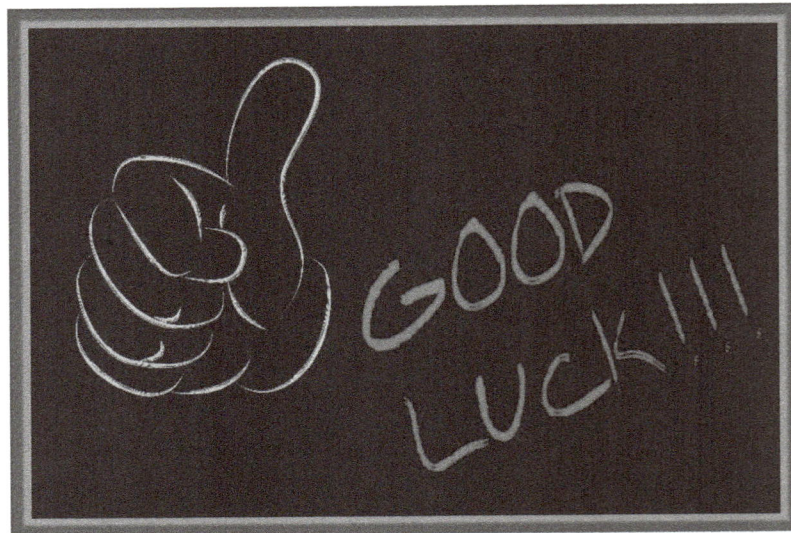

Yes, you need luck and a boatload of patience when Cleopatra and Anthony are teenagers.

If you have been spending a lot of time with them already, you won't need as much luck. But you will still need PATIENCE!!!!

The Teenager

When Cleo and Tony are teenagers and you convince them to spend TIME with YOU, consider yourself blessed.   They may look like they are ignoring you, but they are pleased that you are spending TIME with them.

Listen to Them.

Listening is time very well spent. You will find out things that you need to know. You will find out things that you will have to address at the right time in the right way.

When Cleopatra and Anthony reach this wonderful time in their life, you will have to address many issues. But always focus on spending TIME with them. Then you will get to know the person they have become.

TIME TO
THINK

Why Are the Teenage Years
So Exasperating for Parents?

The teen years are frustrating for a variety of reasons, and even though you were a teenager, the teenagers of today are a different breed than when you were a teenager.

The reasons for their annoying behavior are: their teenage hormones, teenage brains, peers, emotions, and lack of focus.

Scientists have learned that human brains take much longer to fully develop and form than they once thought. The frontal lobe is not as advanced as the rest of the brain. It will catch up with the rest of Anthony's brain in his late twenties. (I know, it is scary, isn't it.)

Researchers discovered that the brain of a teenager takes about 170 milliseconds more time to consider the consequences of their decisions. Unfortunately, this lapse in time makes them more likely to make a riskier decision.

On top of that, their friends or their peers affect their riskiness. As an adult, we don't pick up on the affect that peers have on our teenage children because our brain has matured.

Not only does your teenager have those added milliseconds of extra time to make his decision, his brain also must battle an overpowering force (peers) that signals they should do what feels good.

The Terrible Twos All Over Again

What I am about to tell you is scary. You better sit down.

Even though your 14-year-old looks similar to an adult, rather than a child, Cleopatra's brain has rearranged itself—temporarily—thank goodness— so now your 14-year-old behaves like a two-year-old.

Eventually, their brain will lose some grey matter (sounds counter-intuitive) in the frontal lobe and by the time Anthony is in his 30's, he will behave like an adult again—meaning, he will then have an adult brain.

Emotions of a Teenager

Both Anthony and Cleopatra will go from a super high to a heavy duty low, sometimes within 10 minutes. No, Cleopatra is not a drama queen. Again, researchers have found that teenagers struggle with <u>correctly</u> interpreting the tone of voice and the facial expressions on other people.

Not Your Fault

Most adults know how to interpret facial expressions.

However, Anthony will interpret your disappointed look as ANGER!

As Anthony's brain is already over-stimulated from making a lousy or risky choice, you can expect him to over-react and go on a rampage, like he did as a two-year-old.

What Is Important to Your Teenager

1. They want you to hear them and really LISTEN to them.   Even though we know that the 14-year-old brain has reverted back to the 2-year-old brain, you MUST hear them out. Truly listen. Yes, what they are saying might be total gibberish and poppycock but let them say it. Sometimes when they hear it out loud, they realize their mistakes. Sometimes!

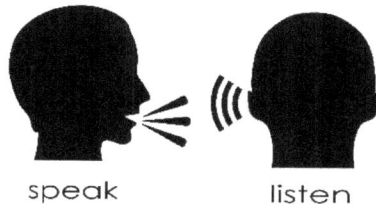

speak   listen

2. Laughter is their best medicine.   Joke with them or give them a joke book, tell some good pun and not so good puns, be self-deprecating and laugh at yourself.

What Is Important to Your Teenager

3. **Teenage** Cleopatra and Anthony are just like their 2-year-old selves. They **want to PLAY!**

4. **Teenagers want to have an adventure!** Who doesn't? But the teenagers need for risk is much higher.

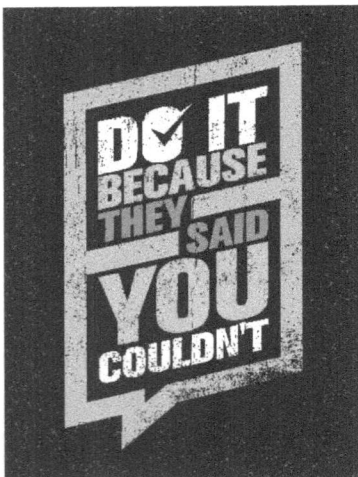

Now that we know how their brain works and what they want to do, let's see what Daddy-Time Tools you can use. (At this point, Anthony most likely will not be calling you Daddy, but Cleopatra might—but not all the time.

The Hang Out House

Make your house the hangout house from the time they are in elementary school and all the way through high school.

You are not doing this because you think you are the only one who can supervise properly or that you don't trust someone else, do it because when Anthony's friends are comfortable with you, then Anthony might not have so many blow-ups.

Don't sit with them and try to be one of the guys—that will assure that no one comes to your house.

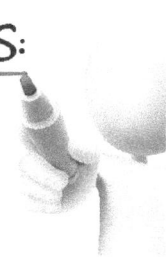

RULES:
1.
2.
3.

Over time Cleopatra's and Anthony's friends will start talking to you. Kids will appreciate that you want them there. They know you have the **same** rules and boundaries that they learned from elementary school.

If you have one rule one week and are mad at Anthony next week and have different rules, it will not work. Be consistent.! It may sound strange, but teenagers appreciate that they are given structure.

Teenagers feel safe with structure.

If your house has been the hangout house for a while, they will feel comfortable with you coming down and talking to them for **_a few minutes._**

That may be all you get, but one day, one of them will ask you a question or ask for advice.

What Do I Do with a Teenager?

This is not a comprehensive list, by any means. These are ideas that might work with Anthony or Cleopatra. Some of them may be totally inappropriate for your child, you know him/her best.

If one of these ideas is something you don't enjoy doing, don't' do it! Cleopatra will see right through you and she will rebel and accuse you of being fake. Then, anything you try to do with her will backfire.

1. <u>Movie Marathon</u>—Anthony or Cleopatra get to pick the movies. Be prepared to be scared because fear lights up the risky part of their brains. Plan to let them stay up. Do not plan to make them get up early because this is what makes it special. Besides, teenagers need more sleep than adults. They will make you suffer if you get them up early. Since you are watching with them, they will be checking to see how brave you are or aren't.

2. <u>Game Night</u>

    Teach them card games. Poker and Blackjack will excite them.

If you play these kinds of games with them, they won't seem so forbidden and therefore more exciting if they first learn them from you. I am sure their friends will want to learn, too.

3. <u>Board Game Marathon</u>

    The same rules apply here as on the Movie Marathon night. If your children do not like board games, then find a video game they can play with you.

4. <u>Play Wii</u>

    Or any sort of physical interactive game. This gets both you and them off the couch. Believe me, these games will tire you out!

What Do I Do with a Teenager?

5. Have a fun "pun" night.

       Puns are jokes that are meant to make people groan, because they usually are awful, but the worse the puns are, the funnier they are.

       A good pun joke starts out with 8 _____ went into the bar, the bartender said he wouldn't serve the 8_____. The 8 _____

replied_____

       Other members of the family must give you what fills in the blank after the number. (You can pick any number you want.)

For example: If 8 cows went into the bar. The bartender said he would not serve the 8 cows. The 8 cows replied _____

       Think about the characteristics of the cow or what you think of when you think about the cow. A cow has an udder. A cow chews a cud. A cow is beef. A cow gives milk.

       Remember, in this game, the pun that gets the most groans is the best.

"The 8 cows replied, "Are you trying to milk the issue?" or

"The 8 cows replied, "That is udderly ridiculous!" or

"The 8 cows replied, "What is your beef?"

       You can choose an occupation, an adjective, a noun, or something that "you would never do" to fill in the blank. Let your kids be creative in choosing what goes in the blank.

6. Stay up late together eating their favorite food. It can be as simple as having a late-night snack together or eating their favorite food while playing games.

7. Karaoke Night--Don't go out and buy a karaoke machine unless this is your passion. Just copy the words to Anthony's songs sing his songs! Write down the words to your songs, and have Anthony sing your songs. You also can try to sing as a duet.

More Teenage Options

8.   <u>Go to a movie together</u> but **travel to a theatre where Cleopatra's friends will not see her.** She will lose her coolness factor if she is seen with her dad. It will be interpreted that she can't find a boyfriend. This is very important, particularly if you have strict rules about dating.

9.   <u>Bowling is a fun activity.</u> Anthony and Cleopatra will enjoy it, but bowling is also something in which you may want to travel to another area. Their biggest fear is that someone will see them. If you are cognizant of this, your children will appreciate you even more.

10.   <u>Play Miniature Golf.</u> Your younger teen will like this more than your older teens.

11.   <u>If you play golf, teach them golf.</u> (Find an inexpensive public course so you won't stress over the fees.) If they enjoy sports, this will give them confidence and will also make them feel special that you are including them in the activities that are important to you.

12.   <u>Go for a walk.</u> Enjoy the fresh air. If there is something they want to talk about, listen. <u>This is not the time to give them a lecture.</u> If you do, they will stop going on walks with you. Enjoy the moment and the exercise.

13.   <u>Read Cleopatra's favorite Young Adult novel</u> and then talk about it over cookies and ice cream. Do not criticize it. Even if you think it is horrible, if she loves it, keep your opinion to yourself! Remember, her brain will interpret your dislike for the book as a dislike of her or her ideas. Tell her what you liked, (there has to be at least one sentence or idea that you liked—no matter how bad it is.), Then tell her what you learned, and/or other insightful opinions.

This will give you another glimpse into the teenage mind.

More Ideas on What to Do with Your Teenager

14. <u>Write a positive note and make it genuine.</u>

If you cannot think of anything positive to write (and there will be days like that) do not write it. It will just make Cleopatra even angrier that you are digging deep to find something positive to say.

Positive Feedback Set

Simply Outstanding! Thank You! Well Done! Loved It!

Perfect Job! Great Work! Too Good! Truly Awesome!

15. <u>Hug Anthony when he is not expecting it</u>. **Do NOT hug him when any friends are around**. Do not hug after an argument—it will seem fake to him and most likely to you, too.

16. <u>Go hiking.</u> Start out simple if you are not a hiker. If you are a hiker let Anthony gradually gain the strength and stamina for the hike before you embark on a long hike. Teenagers can tire quickly, particularly if they had to get up early. **Stop when they are tired**. Do not push them to continue, it will backfire into a huge explosion!

17. <u>Rock Wall Climbing—same as above.</u> If your child is not athletic and you are, don't force the athletics. You may think it will make him feel better, but I have news for you, he won't feel better and just harbor anger that you don't get him.

18. <u>Go Camping.</u> If mom only wants to camp at the Hilton, leave her at home because Cleopatra will pick up her negative vibes and your trip will be for naught.

19. <u>Travel to a location that Anthony wants to visit.</u> Give him parameters. Are you traveling local, state, or overseas? You may want to give him a budget and he gets to choose. This will empower him to problem solve and learn how to budget his money.

Some More Ideas

20.   Go Biking.

21.   Go Swimming.

22.   Play Basketball. Make sure you play with
Cleopatra, too.

23.   Teenagers love adventures so take them on one. Walk around your neighborhood at night
in the dark. (Use your common sense, if your neighborhood is unsafe—do not do this adventure.)
Even though you are walking in the dark, **wear something reflective so cars can see you,** and
hide a small flashlight in your pocket—just in case you need it.

24.   Go Geocaching. Geocaching is a real-world outdoor treasure hunting game. The object of
the game is to hunt for and find objects hidden in a container. There are geocache containers all
over the world. Go to the Geocache website and they will give you the GPS coordinates of
where a "treasure box" is, and then you go find the box.

25.   Find out when there will be a meteor shower
and look at the stars.

26.   In the summer, look for shooting stars.

27. Ask your teenager to teach you something that
they can do, but you don't know how.

Conversation Starters

Sometimes starting a conversation with your teenager can be taxing. You may want to talk, but they have no desire to talk. Don't force them because then it becomes a power struggle. If other people are in the room, you can use a conversation starter and Anthony MAY join in. Teens are usually receptive to conversation when they are eating, and they eat a lot and often! Try these and see what happens.

1.   What is your favorite tradition? Eating a special pastry on a holiday? Traveling to Grandparents every July? Traveling as a family in August? Making special decorations or ornaments? Dad decorates every birthday cake or celebratory cake?

2.   If you could have any super-power, what would you have? Why?

3.   I don't mean to brag, but…. (Tell them something that you are proud of. It doesn't have to be related to anything that your teenager is doing or sports—just something that you feel very good about.)

4   What are the three top things on your bucket list? Why?

5.   What is your favorite time of year? Why?

*Conversation Stopper! ****

*** 6. When your teenager tells you, "I hate it when you_____.
Fill in the blank. Do not defend yourself or become defensive!!!!

Mull it over. How could you fix it?

If it is not fixable, walk away. Don't look angry or hurt—even if you are both angry and hurt.

Discuss this with your child AT A LATER DATE OR TIME.

When you have both calmed down, ask for Cleopatra's or Anthony's input on how to make it better. Do not rush to talk about it, it takes time for your teenager to calm down. You, too!

Your Ideas on What to
Do with Your Teenager

You will come up with ideas of your own. Don't rely on your memory for the next child. This will also be a great help and bring back good memories when you want to pass this book onto Anthony when he becomes a Dad. Make sure you write them down!

_____
_____
_____
_____
_____
_____
_____
_____
_____
_____
_____
_____
_____
_____
_____
_____
_____
_____
_____
_____
_____

You Are Ready, Daddy!

> 66 NEVER LOSE THE PATIENCE - IT'S THE LAST KEY UNLOCKING THE DOOR 99

It is not all fun and games with children and teenagers. They will push your buttons as often as they think they can get away with it.

But the time you have spent and all the fun things that you have done in the previous years, are ingrained in their memories. Believe me, those wonderful memories and your words of wisdom **will** resurface when they need them the most.

Everything that you have done up to now—spending TIME with your child—is frontloading for their teenage years and is training for them when they are a parent.

Be patient! Be patient! Be patient!
Make this your mantra!

> 66 THINGS TAKE TIME. SO JUST BE PATIENT 99

To give you solace, try to remember that in a mere 15 years, when they are in their 30's, they will again be a joy for you, and you can pass this manual on to them.

Sit back and enjoy the ride. You will see that there is no greater happiness than the happiness that a child brings to your life.

When they leave home, you will have lots of time for yourself, and they leave much faster than you think. And during your alone time, you will get to relive those priceless memories. These recollections will stay with you and with your child for the rest of your lives.

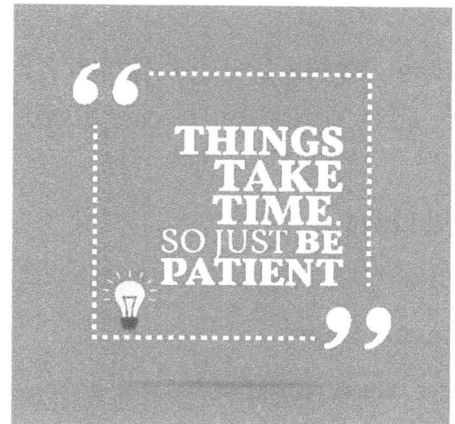

Bibliography

Brain Research

Benjamin, Kathy (2012 February 2) *5 Reasons Teenagers Act the Way They Do*   Retrieved from: http://mentalfloss.com/article/29895/5-reasons-teenagers-act-way-they-do

Weird Laws

Bratskeir, Kate (2016 January 22) *The Craziest Laws that Still Exist in the United States*

Retrieved from:

https://www.huffpost.com/entry/weird-laws-in-america_n_56a264abe4b0d8cc1099e1cd

www.ingramcontent.com/pod-product-compliance
Lightning Source LLC
Chambersburg PA
CBHW08 149040426

42445CB00015B/1818